Red and Blue Play Soccer

Written by Mario Villanueva

Scott Foresman

The red team has on red shirts.

The blue team has on blue shirts.

2   The coach has on a yellow shirt.

The red and blue teams play

soccer. Today is the big game.

Pam is on the blue team.

She hits the ball.

Tim is on the red team.

He runs at the ball.

The blue team runs at it too.   5

Eva is on the blue team.

She kicks the ball.

The blue team kicks the ball in

the net. They score.

Good job, blue team!